Will **Jude** and **Afata** find Elephant Land as they explore Amsterdam?

Join them on this little adventure with their family and learn about all the fun activities you can do there!

BUMBLEBEE PAPERBACK EDITION

Copyright © Sura Hadi 2021

The right of Sura Hadi to be identified as author of
this work has been asserted in accordance with sections 77 and 78 of the Copyright, Designs and
Patents Act 1988.

All Rights Reserved

No reproduction, copy or transmission of this publication
may be made without written permission.
No paragraph of this publication may be reproduced,
copied or transmitted save with the written permission of the publisher,
or in accordance with the provisions
of the Copyright Act 1956 (as amended).

Any person who commits any unauthorised act in relation to
this publication may be liable to criminal
prosecution and civil claims for damage.

A CIP catalogue record for this title is
available from the British Library.

ISBN: 978-1-83934-241-7

Bumblebee Books is an imprint of
Olympia Publishers.

First Published in 2021

Bumblebee Books
Tallis House
2 Tallis Street
London
EC4Y 0AB

Printed in Great Britain

www.olympiapublishers.com

Dedication

**To my inspiring little sister, Layan.**
My little angels: **Jude** and **Elias,** and my big angel **Omar.**
Every moment I spend with you is pure joy.

Thank you **mama.**

# Hi
## my name is Jude

This is my baby brother **Elias**, and **Afata**, my elephant blanket who I call baby. Our dream is to travel to magical places and search for Elephant Land, where we can meet **Afata**'s mommy and daddy. Today we are flying to Amsterdam, the land of canals, flowers, and cheese!

**"Baby, we're going to have lots of adventure in Amsterdam, and maybe we'll find Elephant Land,"** I whisper.

**"Let's go!"** Afata says.

"Canals in Amsterdam are full of floating houses."

"Cool! It's a good thing I can swim!
Afata, Elias, let's climb over the roof to watch the view," I call.

"Wow, I see a lot of colorful houses. They look like cake!" Elias says.
"Jude, Elias, Afata," Daddy calls. "Come down and let's explore!"

"Do you think the ducks in that huge lake will know where Elephant Land is?" I ask Afata.

"Vondelpark is 200 years old," Mommy says. "It's the largest and the most visited park in Amsterdam. I don't think there are any elephants here, but why don't you ask the ducks?

Elias and I have so much fun feeding the ducks and running after them.

The next morning, Mommy wakes us up.
"Rise and shine my little explorers, we have a long day full of surprises!"
"Hurry up boys," Daddy says. "There is no time for breakfast. Let's grab some bitterballen -little Dutch meatballs- from this little corner shop."

"We can then take the tram to the bus stop."
Daddy always knows how to get us anywhere on time.

# THERE ARE WINDMILLS EVERYWHERE

"What are they for?" Elias asks.
"In the past, dutch people used wind power
to mill their grains into flour," Daddy says.
"Like the flour we use to bake cookies with Mommy?" Afata asks Jude

After a few minutes, Mommy points out the window.
"Check out that chocolate factory. It's also from the old days!"
I can smell the chocolate from my window!
Do you think elephants like chocolate?

"I don't think so, I don't see any elephants here," whispers Afata.

Is this our stop? I can't believe my eyes!

# THERE MUST BE MILLIONS OF TULIPS

Let's run through the tulip fields, we can skip, hop and even play hide-and-seek.

**"Daddy, what happens to all these tulips every year?"**
**"They're picked and sold in flower markets around the world,"** Daddy answers.
I pick many colorful flowers and give them to
Mommy because they are beautiful like her.

We choose cargo bicycles with big wagons attached to the back. Afata and I go with Mommy, Elias is with Daddy. The ride is so bumpy, but a lot of fun. Elias and I can't stop laughing as we wave to everyone around us.

We cycle from one canal to another, and up and down the many bridges of Amsterdam. I am surprised at how many different kinds of bicycles I see. Big ones, small ones, long ones, short ones.
**"There are more bicycles in Amsterdam than there are people,"** says Daddy.

We cycle until we get to a huge gate.
"Where do you think we are?" I ask Afata. "The zoo!" Afata says.
"Natura Artis Matistra," Daddy says as he reads the sign above the entrance.
"What does that mean?" I ask.
"It's Latin for 'nature is the teacher of the arts.' This is the oldest zoo in the Netherlands, and one of the oldest zoos in Europe," says Daddy.

i WONDER iF ELEPHANT LAND is iN HERE? LET'S GO!

"**Look, Afata! There are so many different animals!**" but when I turn around, Afata is gone!

"**Afata? Where are you?**" I look everywhere for him. I visit the aquarium where lots of beautiful fish live, but I still can't see him.

I peek through the bushes near the lions' enclosure, but still no Afata. I search around the reindeers' home and even in my Mommy's bag, but I still can't find him. I think we lost Afata forever!

And then I spot him with Elias and Daddy!
"Where did you find him?" I shout.
"We found him next to
the elephants' house," Elias says.
"I thought this was Elephant Land, I was so
excited I got lost," Afata whispers.
"This isnt elephant land, but dont be sad.
We have plenty of time to keep searching.
"Let's cuddle for now. I promise I will never
lose you again!"

The houses look so different from the canals. I like how friends in Amsterdam sit on the canal edges with their legs dangling down. I also love how windows in Amsterdam's old buildings come in so many different shapes and sizes!

The boat man drops us off at a Dutch cheese store.
I found my new favourite cheese and it's gouda! Yum yum.

# TODAY is MUSEUM DAY!

"Have you ever visited a museum before, Afata?
They are full of cool and fun things to do."
First is the NEMO Science Museum, a place where curious people love to go.
Daddy and I did so many experiments and played lots of clever games.
We spend our lunchtime on the rooftop garden.
I look through the telescopes and enjoy beautiful views of Amsterdam!

This is what sailors see from the top of ships! I say to Daddy.
"Sort of, but you'll learn a lot more about ships at the next museum," Daddy replies.
It is the National Martime museum, where we see enormous ships
from the olden days.

"Why did they have so many large ships?" I ask.
"In the past there were no airplanes," Daddy explains. "People used to travel
on ships to get across the ocean. Wanna see what the inside looks like?"
"Yes!" Everything was really old and simple. It is so cool!

**This is our last morning in Amsterdam.**

Daddy promised that we could try some dutch pancakes, which are like normal pancakes, but smaller. We find a good place, and it is worth it!
These are definitely the best pancakes I've ever had.
After breakfast Mommy takes us on an art tour.
There are streets in Amsterdam that are full of art galleries and paintings.
Mommy really loves art, she says it makes you happy.

"Which art museum would you prefer to visit, Daddy?" Mommy asks.
"How about the Van Gogh Museum?
He is one of the most famous Dutch artists," Daddy answers.
Most of the paintings there are about nature and stars.

# THEY ARE FULL OF COLOR & MOVING SKIES!

Before we head back for our last sleep in the boat house, we make one last stop at A'DAM lookout. It's a tall tower on the river with swings on the roof where you can see the whole city from above.

I say goodbye.

**"I think by now we are sure Elephant Land is not in Amsterdam, but this has been a great adventure,"** Afata whispers.

As we are leaving the tower, just outside there is a huge sign that says:
# I amsterdam
"Hurry up everyone. Let's take a photo!" Mommy calls.

As we settle for our last sleep in our little boathouse, I cuddle with Afata.

"Do you think we will ever find elephant land?" Afata whispers.
"Dont worry Afata, there are so many cool places in the world to visit. We are going to have so many more fun adventures, and I'm sure we will find Elephant Land one day, this is just the beginning." I whisper back.

## About the Author

**Sura Abdelhadi** is an architect, an urban designer, a full time mother and a dreamer. She has a great passion for cities and the soul embodied within their physical side. In this travel book series, she directs children's attention to the meaningful details found when visiting a new place. She also opens parent's eyes to see the world through their children's eyes, which creates joy and family bonds out of every little adventure.

**Tarek Abdelkawi** is a graphic designer, illustrator, educator, and a musician with an architectural background. You can see more of his work on Instagram as @minstreldesigns.

Acknowledgement

It takes a creative and a dreamy brain to create images for such a travel book. Therefore, I would like to pay tribute to the incredible artist **Tarek Abdelkawi** who has helped bring this book to life. Finding an artist for this book was a long journey, many thanks.

www.ingramcontent.com/pod-product-compliance
Lightning Source LLC
LaVergne TN
LVHW070451080526
838202LV00035B/2801